D1387802

Sinner

Idea and text by Ben Payne

Sinner

Idea and text by **Ben Payne**
Devised by **Ellie Beedham**, **Ben Payne**, **Liam Steel** and **Rob Tannion**
Realisation **Liam Steel** and **Rob Tannion**

STAN WON'T DANCE

presents

Sinner

Sinner was first performed at Lighthouse, Poole, 5 October 2004 with the following company:

Robert **Liam Steel**
Martin **Rob Tannion**
Direction and Choreography **Liam Steel** and **Rob Tannion**

Set Design **Ruth Finn**
Lighting Design **Ian Scott**
Video **Whitehouse Pictures**
Executive Director **Ellie Beedham** (07973 478325)
Producer **Kerry Andrews**
Assistant Production Manager **Tom Cotterill**
Technical Stage Manager **Matt Spencer**
Press **Bridget Thornborrow** (020 7247 4437)
Advisors **Steve Ehrlischer, Heather Green, Christine Gettins, Peter McGaughin, Gregory Nash, Mark Slaughter, Bridget Thornborrow**

Thanks to
Stuart Hayes and Will Harding for production management advice; Brian Brady, Marie McCluskey and Julia Carruthers for their support; Jane Joyce for her design and photography.

www.stanwontdance.com

Sinner by Stan Wont Dance has been co-commissioned by South Hill Park, Bracknell, The Corn Exchange, Newbury and Swindon Dance. Swindon Dance co-commissioned Sinner as part of the 2004 Taking Risks festival.

Sinner has been made possible with the support of Arts Council England, Laban, South Bank Centre and the Jerwood Space.

Rob Tannion
Joint Artistic Director, Stan Won't Dance
Performer, *Sinner*

Robert Tannion is a London based performer, director and choreographer. He was Dance Artist in Residence at the South Bank Centre and Laban in 2003/04. As a performer and collaborator his work has included DV8 Physical Theatre (1995–2000), Russell Maliphant Company (1998, 2001), Complicité (2002–04) and Klaus Obermaier (2004).
Recent Choreographic Direction includes: *Intent* (Purcell Room, South Bank, London); *Fetish Stories* (City Hall Theatre, Hong Kong 2003); *Dinner* (National Palace of Culture, Sofia 2002); *Q* (Shaw Theatre, London 2003); *Apparition* (Klaus Obermaier – QEH, London, 2004).
Screen credits include: *Stig of the Dump* (BBC 2001, won International Emmy); *Resident Evil* (feature film, 2001); *Function at the Junction* (short, 2001); *flex* (Chris Cunningham short, 2000); *Enter Achilles* (dance film 1996, won an International Emmy).

Liam Steel
Joint Artistic Director, Stan Won't Dance
Performer, *Sinner*

Liam has gained an international reputation as being one of Britain's leading physical theatre practitioners, having directed, choreographed or performed with many of the foremost physical theatre companies in this country. Having originally trained as an actor before moving into dance, he has always been committed to defining new languages for theatre, creating pioneering devised work in the early part of his career with companies such as Ludus Dance Co.; The Kosh and Volcano Theatre Co. For eight years he was a core member of DV8 Physical Theatre as both a performer and Assistant Director of the company. International Tours included *MSM* (Royal Court Co-production); *Enter Achilles* (including the award winning film version); *Bound to Please; The Happiest Day of My Life;* and as designer for *The Cost of Living* (originally commissioned for the cultural festival of the Sydney 2000 Olympic Games). Other freelance performance credits include work with Complicité; David Glass Ensemble; Nigel Charnock and Company; Frantic Assembly; Nottingham Playhouse; The Royal Court; Manchester Royal Exchange; Roundabout Theatre Co; Gay Sweatshop; Theatr Powys; Footloose Dance Company (Powys Dance); Theatre Centre; Soho Theatre and The Royal National Theatre Studio. Recent directorial/ choreographic work includes *The Shooky*, Birmingham Repertory Theatre; *Paradise Lost*, Northampton Theatre Royal; *Pericles,* RSC/Cardboard Citizens Theatre Company; *Strictly Dandia*, Tamasha Theatre Company (with the Lyric Hammersmith and Edinburgh International Theatre Festival); *Devotion*, Theatre Centre; *Frankenstein,* Blue Eyed Soul Dance Company; *Heavenly,* Frantic Assembly/Soho Theatre; (and 2004 Broadway revised version); *Vurt*, Contact Theatre Manchester; *The Fall of the House of Usher*,

GraeaeTheatre Company; *Look at Me,* Theatre Centre; *Hymns*, Lyric Hammersmith/Frantic Assembly; *Sparkleshark*, Royal National Theatre; *The Flight,* Restless Dance Company (Adelaide Festival Theatre-Australia); *15 Degrees and Rising*, Circus Space; *The Secret Garden; Beauty and the Beast; Tom's Midnight Garden, The Ghosts of Scrooge;* Library Theatre, Manchester.

Ellie Beedham
Executive Director, Stan Won't Dance
Ellie has managed a range of projects including festivals, galleries, dance companies and theatres. As a Trustee with Southwark Arts Forum (1998-2003) she focused on regeneration and sustainability through the arts in the London Borough of Southwark, including consultation on Tate Modern, Peckham Library and Laban.
Ellie produced *Jerwood Stairworks 2001*, *Friday is Faraday* (award winning Heritage Festival 2000) and worked with DV8 on the Sydney Olympic Arts Festival Commission *The Cost of Living* (2000). Prior to this, she managed Transitions Dance Company (1997–99). Ellie is an Advisor to the Bonnie Bird Choreography Fund and on the Board of Directors of Kaos Theatre. She specialises in branding and communications, rebranding the Lyric Hammersmith in 2001/02 and is currently Head of Communications at Laban.

Kerry Andrews
Producer
Kerry Andrews is the Producer of Stan Won't Dance. She trained in dance, and later graduated in Arts Practice & Cultural Policy. She has worked with a range of companies internationally, including Rambert Dance Company, Akram Khan Company, Fabulous Beast Dance Theatre and Mavin Khoo Dance. Currently her other clients include Rafael Bonachela who choreographed Kylie Minogue's *Fever* tour.
Kerry also worked as an Arts Officer for Local Government, as a Dance Officer for the Arts Council of England, and as a manager for the 2002 master series programme with John O'Connell (choreographer on *Moulin Rouge* film) for Ausdance NSW and Sydney Dance Company.

Ben Payne
Writer
Ben Payne is an Associate Director of Birmingham Repertory Theatre with particular responsibility for new writing and the programme of The Door, the Rep's space for new work. For the company he has previously written the stage adaptation of Jim Crace's novel *Quarantine*, directed by Bill Alexander (2000), an adaptation of Bertolt's Brecht's *The Wedding* (2001) and is currently writing a new play for young people based on Camille Saint-Saens orchestral piece, *The Carnival of the Animals*. Another play for young people *The Last Laugh* has been performed by youth theatres in Britain, South Africa and Thailand. His screenplay *On a hiding to nothing*,

written with excluded students at Lindsworth School and directed by Saul Hewish, premiered at the 2002 Birmingham Film Festival. He is also currently working on *Darkness*, a comedy about the last eunuch in Britain.

Ruth Finn
Set Design

Ruth Finn studied Theatre Design and Realisation at Croydon College. Design and Realisation includes: *Theseus and The Minotaur, Off The Wall, Unheimlichspine* and *The Chimp That Spoke* with The David Glass Ensemble, *The Blue Remembered Hills* with Yellow Earth, *Presto* with Group K, *Taylor's Dummies* with Gecko, *Tempest* directed by Kate Beales and Sue Buckmaster, *Playing From The Heart* for Polka Theatre and *Find Me* with Indelible Theatre Company. Current designs include UK Tours *Disembodied*, directed by David Glass and Tom Morris and *Bent* with Graeae.

Ruth also works as an artist and is co-founder of Tandem, a cross arts facilitation company.

Ian Scott
Lighting Design

Recent work: *Observe The Sons of Ulster...* (Abbey Theatre), *Two Step* (Almeida Theatre), *Slamdunk* (Nitro), *8000m* (Suspect Culture), *Bad Girls* (Watershed / Polka Theatre) *Arcane...* (Opera Circus) and *Warrior* (London Planetarium).

Other theatre credits include: *Oh What a Lovely War* (Royal National Theatre), *Savoy* (Peacock Theatre), *Skeletons of Fish* (LIFT), *The Chimp That Spoke* (David Glass Ensemble), *Frogs* (Cottesloe, RNT), *The Lament for Arthur Cleary* (7:84), *Stalinland* (Citizens Theatre), *Taylors Dummies* (Gecko), *Peeling* (Graeae), *Henry IV* (Abbey Theatre), *The Beauty Queen of Leenane* (Tron Theatre), *Blown* (Theatre Royal, Plymouth) and *Crazy Horse* (Paines Plough). Ian is an Associate Artist of Suspect Culture and a regular collaborator with Nitro, Opera Circus and the pioneering theatre company Graeae.

Tom Cotterill
Assistant Production Manager

Tom read English and Theatre Arts at Goldsmiths', specialising in Scenography, Stage, Touring and Technical Management. Credits include *One in A Million* (Theatre Alibi), *Rabbit* (Frantic Assembly), *The Chimp That Spoke* (David Glass Ensemble), *Presto* (Group K), *Sealboy: Freak* (Mat Fraser), *I Am The Walrus* (Nabil Shaban) and *The Piranha Lounge* (Dende Collective). Worked as Set Designer on *Talking About Men* and *Juniors Story* (Steven Luckie and Oval House), *Sacrificed* (Spirit2Reality), *Coming Up For Air* (Crescent Theatre), *Under Their Influence* (Theatre Kushite) and on *The Canterville Ghost* (Theatre Buddha / Illpalchettostage).

Matt Spencer
Technical Stage Manager

Matt trained in dance at Bretton Hall where he received choreographic commissions from the East of England Orchestra, Worcester and Derby County Councils and several contemporary dance companies. Upon graduating in 1999 he established Compound Productions where he developed the use of interactive media in live performance and directed three physical theatre productions for UK tours. Matt is an experienced 2D and 3D digital animator, and currently works with London-based physical theatre companies producing real-time video and performance interactive. Recently Matt's worked with Gekko (*Taylor's Dummies, The Race*), Lunasea (*Moon Behind Clouds*) and is a member of the David Glass Ensemble, working as video artist for productions (*The Chimp that Spoke, Disembodied*) and facilitator on International Lost Child Projects.

Sinner

a self-destructive solo for two men

First published in 2004 by Oberon Books Ltd.
(incorporating Absolute Classics)
521 Caledonian Road, London N7 9RH
Tel: 020 7607 3637 / Fax: 020 7607 3629
e-mail: oberon.books@btinternet.com
www.oberonbooks.com

A catalogue record for this book is available from the British Library.

ISBN: 1 84002 498 4

Cover photographs: Jane Joyce

Printed in Great Britain by Antony Rowe Ltd, Chippenham.

Introduction

In April 1999, three different areas of London were subject to nail-bomb attacks: Brixton Market, Brick Lane and Soho. In each case, the areas were targeted because they were seen as focal points of the Afro-Caribbean, Asian and gay communities of London. The first bomb caused many injuries, the second caused few, but only because it had inadvertently been planted on a day when the local market did not run. The third bomb was left in a bag in the Admiral Duncan Pub in Old Compton Street on the evening of Friday 30 April. The explosion caused 3 deaths and injured over 80 people. David Copeland, the perpetrator of all three attacks, was arrested later the same evening. Despite pleading manslaughter on the grounds of diminished responsibility at his trial, he was convicted of murder and given six life sentences.

Sinner should not been seen as documentary or biography but as a piece of theatre partly inspired by these events.

1

A man stands on the platform
Of an ordinary suburban railway station,
This man.

At his feet, a neatly packed holdall –
As if you could pack up your whole life
Into one bag and
Leave it all for good,
As if you could.

Witnesses on that particular night
Report seeing
A tall man,
A short man,
That he was dark,
That he was fair,
But that there was this man
And that he took this journey
There is no doubt.

And on the train into the city,
Everyone he sees looks
Stranger, stronger, brighter,
Everyone he sees looks
Like a monster to him.
And everyone he sees, he thinks,
Knows
Exactly where he's going and
Exactly what he's going to do,
As if they could see straight through him
As if he was just a pane of sweating glass.

So what did he look like...
This sweating man?
Did you sit next to him on that particular night?
Were you ever close to him?
Did you happen to catch his eye and smile?
Or look away

At all the many other reflections
Glancing
Back and forth
In that particular carriage,
On that particular night?

Well?
Is that his face?
Is that the kind of face that you would remember?
Can you put a name to that face?
Is that the face of an angel? A liar? A lover? A monster?
Fanatic or fantastic fuck...?

And in the city now,
The cameras catch his every angle,
All his endless possibilities:
A tall man,
A short man,
A dark man,
A fair man,
Walking
To a certain part of town,
To a certain street,
To a certain bar

Where he stands outside for quite for some time
As if deliberating.

Go on.
Do it.

You can be who you want to be.
Exactly who you want to be...

And so a man walks into a bar,
This man,
This man walks into a bar,
To have a drink,
To have a life,
To make a little mayhem.

And the moment he goes through that door
He could be anyone.

2

ROBERT walks through the door of a bar with a bag.

Robert
So, is this how it happens?
One night you arrive.
One night you're not there
The next you are.
It's as simple as that.

When you first arrive
You are probably carrying a bag and wearing the wrong
clothes.
(Never mind all those hours that you thought about what you
were going to wear,
You are very clearly wearing the wrong clothes...)

And as you stand in the door
It feels like everyone is looking at you
Even though they're not.
And you just wish you could be somewhere else
But you aren't.

You wish this could have happened at a better time
But it couldn't.
You wish you could have been a different person
But you can't.
And most of all, you wish you could say sorry
To everyone, for everything, for all of it
Before any of it happens.
Because whatever happens, it's too late now, you've arrived,
so...

Do not look left.
Do not look right.
And above all don't look at anyone straight in the face.

And because you think it must be important to look as if you
belong here

You try to look like someone who knows exactly where they're
going and exactly what they're going to do.
Try to avoid the strange man who seems to be dancing with
the fag machine.
Try to look *cool*...

Do not look right.
Do not look left.

And, above all, mind those fucking steps.

And then you've arrived.
Well –
You've arrived at the bar.

And so you look around
And then you notice
Him.
And so you look away.
And when you look back
To see if he's noticed
You
You try not to look as if you've noticed the fact
That he clearly looks
As if he's trying to look
As if he hasn't noticed
You.

And then taking your coca-cola
And swerving to avoid Fag Machine Man again
Who now seems to want to dance with *you*...
NO I'M NOT
I'M NOT DANCING!
CAN'T YOU SEE?

I'M NOT DANCING!

...you go and find yourself a place
And sit.
Where you notice

For one moment
What looks like the face of a friend,
Before you realise
It's just your own face
Looking back at you.
And you –

And there you sit
And you listen to the music.
And you sit
And

You sit
And you sit
You sit and wait.

Even though sitting and waiting here feels strange.
And you don't know why.
And you won't know why it feels strange today
Because you've only just got here, remember?

But one day you will know
That it was strange because you felt
Right where you belong and also
As if you'd just hung yourself from a meat-hook.

So you wonder
Is this how it happens?

And for many nights you're wondering
Is this how it happens?
When one night it happens.

    MARTIN comes through the door with a bag.

One night, he's not there, the next he is.
And as he stands in the door, he is clearly wearing the right
clothes.
And he looks like everyone is looking at him.
And he doesn't look left and he doesn't look right.
And, above all, he doesn't look anyone straight in the face.

He just looks like somewhere who knows exactly where he's
going
And exactly what he's going to do.

ROBERT looks at MARTIN.

It's as simple as that.

And so you sit and wait
And wonder
Does an angel – ?

MARTIN looks at ROBERT.

Is this how it happens?

3

MARTIN approaches ROBERT.

Martin
Is this seat taken?

Hello?

Is this seat taken?

Robert
What? Sorry?

Martin
Is this seat taken?

Robert
Yeah. It's fine

Martin
What?

Robert
No, it isn't.

Martin
It isn't taken? Or it isn't fine?

Robert
Yeah.

I mean, no.

No. No-ones sitting there. No.

Martin
Fantastic. Thanks.

MARTIN sits.

You ok, mate?

I said, 'you ok, mate'?

Robert
Fine thanks.

…You?

Martin
I'm fantastic.

Thanks very much for asking.

Having a good time yet?

Robert
Yeah, fantastic time, thanks.

Martin
So what do you think of the décor in here?

Robert
What?

Martin
The *décor?*

Robert
The what?

Martin
What do you think?

Robert
In here?

Martin
In *here*.

Robert
The *décor*?

Martin
Yeah.

Robert
What do *you* think?

Martin
I think it's fucking fantastic.

You know that kind of raw, stripped-back, industrial look?
Up there above the bar?
All those pipes and rivets and
…shit.
See? Fantastic.
They've really gone to town, haven't they?

Robert
Yeah. They have.

It's alright, yeah.

Martin
I'm sorry. Am I bothering you? Were you *waiting* for someone?

Robert
I'm waiting for my – boyfriend.

Martin
Oh. OK. Your —
What time is // he — ?

Robert
He's late.

Martin
Does he usually keep you waiting?

Robert
Who?

Martin
Your boyfriend?

Robert
Oh. Yeah, usually.

No. Not usually, no.

Martin
OK, so am I or am I not bothering you?

Robert
No you're alright, mate, honest. Whatever. Do whatever you like, yeah?

Martin
Great. Thanks. I will.

I get this feeling that this might be your first time here, right?

Me too.
Takes some guts, doesn't it?
Just to come in straight off the street into a strange place on your own.
I get this feeling you've wandered around for ages beforehand
Not really knowing what to do.

Feeling a bit of a spare prick, in fact.

Robert
Oh yeah? How can you tell that?

Martin
Well, there's the way you're stuck to that seat for starters.
And you look really red in the face too?
You know, sort of – *hypertensive?*

Robert
Yeah? Right...

Martin
And that's no good, is it? I mean, you've gotta have bigger
plans for the evening than sticking in that seat, right?

Robert
Right.

Martin
...Or you might just as well as have stayed at fucking
home...

Robert
I'm fine.
I'm fine just sitting here.
Really, *alright.*

It's just you look in the doors of these places sometimes
And you see all these people having fun
And you wonder what's going on.
Then one night you think: I can just go in.
What's stopping me?
So that's what I did.
I just came in.

Martin
It's ok, mate. It's fine. I was once in your place, remember?

Martin

My name's Martin, by the way.

Robert
Robert.

Martin
Pleased to meet you.

Robert
Martin.

Martin
Robert.

Robert
Pleased to meet you. Martin...

Martin
Pleased to meet you...

Robert
Robert.

Martin
Martin.

Robert
Martin.

Both
Pleased to meet you.

Martin
My name's Martin, by the way. Pleased to meet you.

MARTIN takes ROBERT's hand. ROBERT flinches.

Hey, it's ok, I do this a lot.

I do this all the time.

You go into a bar
To have a drink.
To have a life.

To make a little mayhem.

It's a natural fucking urge.

And when you're in there with all those bodies close to yours…
When the whole place feels like it's dancing
Dancing for you,
And you smell their sweat
You smell their breath…
You're in paradise

Because to lose a little of yourself
Now and then,
To feel like someone else
Took your place for the night
Feels like paradise to me.

How about you?

And when you wake up
You wonder
Was that me? Did I do all those things?
And then you remember –
Yes
That was me.
All of it was me.

So
Is it written all over me?
Is it written on my face?
All the sordid details of my secret, sinful life?

Well, *probably*…

But then we're these perfect creatures, my friend
Who should be out having a good time.
And who can stop us?
Who's going to stop us having a good time?

By the way
Did I say?
My name's Martin, by the way.
Pleased to meet you.

Robert
Robert. My name is Robert.
Pleased to meet you.

Martin
Listen, mate, I'd like to buy you a drink. Would you like a drink?

Robert
OK.

Martin
What would you like to drink?

I would like to buy you a drink.

Robert
Thanks.

Martin
Would you like a drink?

Robert
OK

Martin
What would you like to drink, mate?

Robert
I'll have a pint of blood, please.

Martin
I don't think they do that here, mate, er –

They do –

// Beer

Robert
Beer.

Yeah, I meant beer. I'll have a pint of *beer* please.

Sorry – I'm just not used to – you know...

Martin
Hey it's ok. It's fine. Really...
Didn't I say? I was once in your place.

   MARTIN's phone rings.

Hello?

Hello?

Who is this?

Who are you?

I think you've got the wrong person

I'm just not that sort of person

I'd never do anything to harm anyone

No

No

Never

Never

No

Listen, I want you to think of me as a friend.

And I am your friend

But, listen, you have to understand

I can't do this –

I don't *hate* you

It's just that I can't listen

I can't listen to this

I can't listen –

I can't listen to any of it anymore

I can't

I can't

Listen

To you

Any

More

So I'm going to go

You're going to have to go

Please

Just leave me alone

Leave me alone

Just who the fuck do you think you are?

MARTIN ends the call.

Robert
Robert.

My name is Robert.

Martin
So, Robert, what gym do you go to?

Robert
What?

MARTIN picks up ROBERT's bag.

Martin
The bag...
I've got one just like it.
You can get a whole lot in them, can't you?

Robert
Yeah, that's right. You can.

Martin
So what's in yours?

Robert
Nothing.

Martin
Nothing?

Robert
Just clothes.

Martin
Just clothes?

Robert
Just clothes

Martin
What sort of clothes?

Robert
Just *clothes.*

Martin
You know, I'm kind of getting the impression that you're quite a closed person...

Robert
Are you? Yeah?

Martin
Yeah. Whereas I'm blessed with being very open...

Robert
Are you? Yeah?

Martin
Yeah.

ROBERT retrieves his bag from MARTIN.

Robert
No offence, right? But you could be // anyone.

Martin •
That's right: I could be anyone.

And you could be anyone.

You can be who you want to be.
Exactly who you want to be...

So why don't we find the real you, then?

Robert
What?

Martin
And maybe then you can find the real me.

Robert
OK

Martin
So...
Are you a light person or a heavy person?
A much-loved person or a much-unloved person?
A glass half-full person or a glass half-empty person?
A generally happy, easy-going, outgoing, people-type of
person,
Or a withdrawn, miserable, whacked-out, fucked-up, cunty-
type of person?

Robert
I'm nothing... I'm – just nothing –

Martin
OK...

Robert
OK, no offence, right, but I'm gonna – gonna leave, yeah?

I'm gonna – I've gotta go – find a bank

It's late – and // I'm

ROBERT looks at his watch.

Martin
I'm sorry. Am I bothering you?

Robert
No, it's just // that...

Martin
Were you *waiting* for someone?

Robert
I don't know.

Martin
Well, it looks as if they're not coming, doesn't it?

Robert
Yes.

Martin
OK. So am I or am I not bothering you?

Robert
No. Yes. I don't know.

Martin
I think
You need to relax a bit more.
Maybe smile a bit more.
I think you might like to be a happier person.
That you might like the possibility of being happy...

Isn't that right?

Robert
...I might.

Martin
So, do you dance?

Robert
What?

Martin
Do you dance?

Robert
No.

Martin
Oh, ok.

So you don't dance?

Robert
No.

Martin
Why not?
You should dance.

   MARTIN begins dancing.

Everybody should dance.
What do they say?
'Love like you've never been hurt,'
'Dance like nobody's watching'
And
And
Do something else like I can't fucking remember.

But dance like nobody's watching.
Because that's how you dance.
By not caring
By forgetting yourself.

Robert
I won't dance, mate.

Martin
Don't you believe in people having fun?

Robert
Yeah.

Well, I suppose I do.

It's just that when I look in the doors of these places sometimes, I wonder what's going on.

The world turns,
There's so much pain,
And you're all just – having fun.

Martin
But one night you thought 'I can just go in,
What's stopping me?'
And that's what you did.
You just came in.

Robert
Yeah.

But I won't dance, mate.

Martin
It's ok. I wasn't asking you to.

My family were never big on dancing.

Robert
Nor were mine.

Martin
In fact, my parents were quite religious

Robert
So were mine.

Martin
They taught me the difference between right and wrong –

Robert
That virtue was its own reward –

Martin
And the true meaning of sacrifice –

Robert
Right.

Martin
Right.

Not that I've paid attention to any of that shit since, mind…

What about you?

Robert
What about me?

Martin
Do you believe in God?

Robert
I'd like to.
I'd like to think –
There's an Order…

Martin
So do you believe in Destiny?
I mean, do you believe that us meeting tonight was, like,
Fate?

Robert
Some people believe that.

Martin
Right. Some people believe there's some way, some // where,
someone

Robert
Somewhere, someone, where they were always heading, no
matter what…

Martin
And it was always going to happen.

Robert
No matter what

Yeah.

And there are other people that think life is just Random

Martin
Just Total Fucking Chaos

Maybe with a few Edited Highlights thrown in

Robert
Just to keep us all watching.

Martin
Just to keep us all sane.

So what do you think?

Robert
I'd like to –

I think I'd like to believe that good things happen for good people.
And that bad things happen to bad people.

Martin
Fantastic.
I'd like to believe that too.
You know, I think any kind of religion is great
As long as it doesn't involve actively harming people, of course.

So which are you?

Robert
Which religion am I?

Martin
No. Which are you, Robert?

A good person or a bad person?

Robert
I'm –

Martin
You're – ?

Robert
I –

Martin
You – ?

Robert
I'm –

ROBERT extends his hand.

...Pleased To Meet You

MARTIN and ROBERT dance.

So, do you go out dancing a lot then?

Martin
What do you mean?

Robert
You know – clubbing, parties. You do that a lot then, do you?

Martin
What you really mean is 'do I take a lot of drugs and sleep around?'

Robert
No, I don't.

Martin
Yes, you do.

Robert
I'm not judging you.

Martin
Yes, you are.

Robert
OK, I am.

Martin
I'm a single man, Robert. I can do whatever and whoever I like, can't I?

Robert
Yes, you can.

Martin
What do you think? Do you think taking drugs is a matter of informed personal choice?

Robert
I suppose so, yeah.

Martin
And do you think someone can be truly happy all of the time?

Robert
Some of the time you can.

Martin
But all of the time?

Robert
Maybe not all of the time, no.

Martin
And if you can't be truly happy all of the time.
What else is there but having fun?

Robert
I don't know

Martin
But then you can't have *sex* all of the time either, can you?

Robert
No, you can't.

Martin
I mean, you'd have to be not right up there
Or down here,
To think that, wouldn't you?

Robert
Yes, you would.

Martin
And if there's no happiness
No fun,
No sex
All of the time
What else is there?

Robert
I don't know.

Martin
I mean, I'm not some kind of addict, right?
These things haven't got control of me.

Robert
You've got control of them...

Martin
Right.

And as for drugs –

Robert
What about drugs?

Martin
I truly believe they've made me a better, nicer person.

Robert
Do you?

Martin
Oh yeah. I do.

So do you want to take some drugs, Robert?

Robert
No, I'm alright thanks.

Martin
Well, that's just fine. That's a matter of informed personal choice.

*MARTIN's phone rings. MARTIN stops dancing.
ROBERT dances.*

Hello?

And who are you?

Who the fuck *are* you?

Are you my brother?

Are you my dad?

Are you God?

Are you this little nagging voice in my head I hear

Wherever I go, whatever I do

No, no, no, no, no

I'll tell you who you are

You're a liar

You're a disease

You're my disease

You're my worst fucking nightmare

You're everything and anything that there is to blame

You're every bad fucking thing that ever happened to me.

You're a piece of shit

You're nobody

Yeah

Yeah

Yeah? Well you know what?

Well, perhaps you should take a look at yourself sometimes.

ROBERT watches MARTIN. MARTIN watches ROBERT.
MARTIN ends the call. ROBERT stops dancing.

Robert
Is this my bag?

Martin
Yeah.

Robert
Or yours?

Martin
Yours.

Robert
Are you sure?

Martin
Yeah.

Robert
Are you sure they didn't get swapped around?

Martin
Like when?

Robert
Like when you were on the phone or something?

Martin
Positive. Why?

Robert
It's just that you can't be too careful with that kind of thing nowadays.

Martin
What do you mean?

Robert
You know what I mean.

Martin
What are you accusing me of? Don't accuse me // of something that I haven't done

Robert
I'm not accusing you of anything. Listen, // I'm sorry

Martin
Yeah listen, I'm sorry, I think there's been some kind of // mix-up here –

Robert
Yeah, listen, I'm sorry

I'm sorry.

I'm a bit – just a bit

Just a bit all over the place…

Martin
Hey it's ok. Didn't I say? I was once in your place.

MARTIN goes to kiss ROBERT. ROBERT moves away.

Jesus. You really need someone looking after you, don't you?

I don't even know what's in that bag, mate.

Robert
I told you – nothing... //
Just clothes.

Martin
Like you said,
Just clothes.

And why would I want to steal your clothes?

Would you want to steal mine...

MARTIN extends his hand.

Robert...?

Robert
Martin. Pleased to meet you.

Martin
Robert.

Robert
Pleased to meet you...

Martin
Pleased to meet you.

Robert
Robert.

Martin
Martin.

Robert
Martin.

Both
Pleased to meet you.

BEN PAYNE

Martin
Are you ok, mate?

Robert
What?

Martin
I said, 'Are you, ok, mate...?'

Robert
I'm −

Fine, thanks.

You?

Martin
Fantastic. Thanks very much for asking.
Having a good time yet?

Robert
Fantastic time, thanks.

ROBERT looks at his watch.

Martin
I'm sorry. Am I bothering you?

Robert
No − it's just // that −

Martin
Were you *waiting* for someone?

Robert
I'm waiting for my boyfriend.

Martin
Well, it looks like they're not coming, doesn't it?

Robert
Yes

Martin
So you can stay for another drink then?

Robert
No. I don't know. Yes.

Martin
There you go, we're having fun now aren't we?

Robert
Yes.

Martin
Because otherwise you might as well have stayed at fucking home, right?

Robert
Yes.

Martin
Because you've gotta have bigger plans for the evening than sticking to that seat, right?

Robert
Yes.

Martin
Because we're these perfect creatures, my friend,
Who should be out having a good time.
And who can stop us?
Who's going to stop us having a good time?

4

Later.

MARTIN is singing loudly.

Robert
– sing like no-one's listening...

Martin
What?

Robert
That's the other one – dance like no-one's looking, love like you've never been hurt.

Sing like no-one's listening

Martin
Are you taking the piss?

Robert
What? No, mate, // honest.

Martin
Are you taking the fucking piss?

Robert
No, mate. Honest, no. Not at all.

Martin
OK.

You know what? You think I'm your mate.
And you know what?
I think I am your mate.
But maybe not in the way that you think I'm your mate.

Robert
OK

Martin
But you're having a good time, yeah?

Robert
Fantastic time, yeah, thanks.

It's just you look in the doors of these places sometimes and you wonder...

Everyone's so mixed up, aren't they?

Everyone's so fucked up...

Martin
In a nice way, though.

Robert
Yeah, fucked up in a *nice* way –

Martin
But still totally fucked // up.

Robert
Totally fucked up

Everyone is so mixed up and fucked up nobody knows who or what the fuck they are anymore, do they?

Martin
No – too right, mate. I'm with you on that one.

And this could be a really nice place, couldn't it?

Without all these fucked up people fucking the place up.

And I'll tell you who else I really hate too...

Robert
Who?

Martin
Fat people

Robert
Yeah...?

Martin
Grossly fat people and
Anyone with bad hygiene.
I mean, there's no excuse these days, is there?

Robert
Anyone with spots.

Martin
Spots.

Or big glasses.

OK, no offence right, and I know it's a medical condition, but big glasses just don't do it for me.

I couldn't ever sleep with someone with big glasses. They just don't do it for me.

Robert
Nor me.

Martin
Or effeminate people.

Robert
Try-hards, wannabes, saddos of any description.

Losers.

Martin
Right, losers...

Robert
Nobodies.

Martin
Nobodies.

Anyone really fucked up.

Robert
Anyone really badly fucked up –

Martin
Yeah.

Robert
Really hairy people.

Martin
People with hairy feet in particular.

Robert
I hate

Liars.

Martin
Limpets.

Robert
Luvvies.

Martin
Hippies.

Robert
Students.

Martin
Christians.

Robert
Arty-farty layabouts.

Martin
Belgians.

Robert
Arabs.

Martin
Gypsies.

Robert
Women.

Martin
Short-arses.

Robert
Are you taking the piss?

Martin
What? No, mate. No. Honest.

I hate

Anyone whose face doesn't fit, in fact.

There are too many of them

And too few of us.

And you know what I say?

Robert
Clear them all out.

Martin
They all deserve what's coming to them, don't they?
I really really fucking hate

Anyone who mucks around with kids.

Robert
Sickos.

Martin
Degenerates.

Robert
I hate

Perverts.

Martin
Murderers.

The mentally ill.

I hate them all.

Nail them all.

Kill them all.

Except no-one these days has got the guts to say it

Or do it, have they?

Have they?

No one...

Robert
Are you taking the piss?

Martin
What? No. No, mate, honest.

Not at all.

I'm just asking.

I'm just asking –

Do you hate *me*?

Robert
What?

Martin
It's a simple question. Do you hate me?

Because it's a simple feeling: hate.

But if you grow up in an ordinary suburban family –

Mum, Dad, Gran, brother, sister, dog. Ordinariness.
Nothingness. Where England expects // nothingness

Robert
Nothingness.

Martin
...there's nothing much to hate, is there?

And when you hear your Mum talk about you, it's always as –

Robert

– the gentle one, the loving one.

Martin

Because there's nothing there to hate.

But the world always feels like a cartoon to you. Colours too bright, the sound too high. Mum and Dad laughing too loud.

Robert

At what? At you?

Martin

About what?

Robert

You don't know

Martin

You think –

Robert

You guess –

Martin

But you don't know...

Robert

Because there's nothing there

Martin

No, there's nothing there to –

But
Somehow – they know – and you know –

Robert

You're going wrong. You can feel yourself

Martin

Just going wrong.

They take the piss out of you at school.

The fat one.

Robert
The runty one.

Martin
The quiet one

Robert
The sensitive one.

But that's not it.

Martin
No. That's not it.

Robert
You just feel like a nothing, a nobody. And when you look –

Martin
There's nothing there. And nobody wants to be a nobody. Everybody wants to be a somebody, don't they, my friend?

Because if no-one remembers who you were, you never existed.

Robert
Right.

Martin
So that's when you really start to go off the rails. You start hanging around with the wrong sort of crowd. That's when you really find out about hate.

Robert
No.

Martin
Yes. That gives you something to believe in, a purpose, some kind of order, doesn't it?

Robert
No.

Martin
But it's the emotion really. To *feel* something about other people even if it's hate *feels* like – something.

Robert
No.

Martin
Just to have something *felt* about you – even if it's hate – *feels* like something.

Robert
No.

Martin
You think you can get away from these feelings.
But whenever you look
They're there.
They're always there.
It's this monster following you.
About to catch you.
About to swallow you up.

His face is the one that's in all the newspapers.
His face is the one that's on TV.
The one that won't ever let you go.

But then one morning you wake up:
And you're a man on an ordinary suburban railway platform
A packed bag at your feet.

And you take that bag
To a place where people enjoy themselves
And you –

Robert
What?

Martin
Boom.

You're on TV. You're somebody.

You're there.

It's as simple as that.

And, you know what? Good on you – they all deserved to fucking die.

MARTIN's phone rings.

Hello?

Hello?

Robert
(*To MARTIN.*)
Hello?

Who is this?

Who are you?

I think you've got the wrong person

I'm not that sort of person

I'd never do anything to harm anyone

No

No

Never

Never

No

I *don't* hate you

I want you to think of me as a friend.
And I am your friend

I *don't* hate you

But you have to understand

I can't do this

I can't do it

I *don't hate* you but

I can't listen to this

I can't listen to you

I can't listen to you

I can't listen to any of it anymore

You have to go

You have to go

I'm going to have to make you go

I'm going to have to make you fucking

Go

Now

Please

Leave me alone

Please just leave me the fuck alone

Martin
Hello?

Hello?

Who is this?

Who is this?

   MARTIN ends the call, disorientated.

Is this my bag?

Robert
Yeah...

Martin
Or yours?

Robert
Yours

Martin
Are you sure?

Robert
Positive. Why?

Martin
Are you sure they didn't get swapped around?

Robert
Like when?

Martin
Like when I was on the phone or something?

Robert
You've never been on the phone.

Martin
No...you're right.

It's just that you can't be too careful with that kind of thing
nowadays.

Robert
What do you mean?

Martin
You know what I mean.

Robert
Are you accusing me of something? Don't accuse me of
something // I haven't done.

Martin
So you didn't spike my bag?

Robert
Spike your // – bag??

Martin
Yeah, no, sorry, // listen there's been a –

Robert
Listen, // I think –

Martin
Listen, I'm sorry.

Robert
I think there's been some kind of misunderstanding here –

We've already had this // conversation, OK?

Martin
Yeah. Yeah. Listen, I'm sorry.

I'm sorry.

I'm a bit – just a bit

All over the place...

Robert
I don't even know what's in that bag, mate.

Martin
I told you //
Just *clothes.*

Robert
Like you said: just clothes.

And why would I want to steal your clothes?

Would you want to steal mine?

Jesus. You really need somebody looking after you, don't you?

Hey, it's ok. Didn't I say? I was once in your place. Remember?

ROBERT goes to kiss MARTIN. MARTIN lashes out.

OK. No offence, right but I'm gonna gonna leave, yeah? I'm gonna – I've gotta go – find a bank.

He looks at his watch.

It's late and – I'm – It's just that I'm just finding you – finding you a bit – you know. I dunno. I dunno what it is. But I just think I should, I should go. I really shouldn't have come in here in the first place. You're a nice bloke, yeah? But I'm finding this all a bit – messy. It's too messy. Yeah. It's me. Not you. I'm – a mess. Yeah. That's what I am.

Martin
(*Overlapping.*)
OK. No offence, right but I'm gonna gonna leave, yeah? I'm gonna – I've gotta go – find a bank.

He looks at his watch.

It's late and – I'm – It's just that I'm just finding you – finding you a bit – you know. I dunno. I dunno what it is. But I just think I should, I should go. I really shouldn't have come in here in the first place. You're a nice bloke, yeah? But I'm finding this all a bit – messy. It's too messy. Yeah. It's me. Not you. I'm – a mess. Yeah. That's what I am.

Robert
(*Overlapping.*)
OK. No offence, right but I THINK YOU'RE FUCKING WEIRD. I'm gonna – I've gotta get THE FUCK RIGHT OUT OF HERE cos I'm finding you – finding you a bit LIKE A FUCKING PSYCHO I dunno. I dunno what it is. I should – I SHOULD NEVER HAVE FUCKING COME IN HERE IN THIS FUCKING SHIT-HOLE IN THE FIRST PLACE. You're a –

you're a nice bloke, NOT A NICE FUCKING BLOKE, RIGHT, YOU'RE A LOSER, A FUCKING TOSSER, so don't fucking MESS WITH ME, DON'T FUCKING MESS WITH ME, RIGHT? DON'T FUCKING MESS WITH MY HEAD.

5

ROBERT overpowers MARTIN.

Robert
You're my brother.

You're my dad.

You're God.

You're the little nagging voice in my head..

Wherever I go, whatever I do...

You're a liar.

You're a disease.

You're my disease.

You're my worst fucking nightmare.

You're everything and anything that's to blame.

You're every bad thing that ever happened to me.

You're a piece of shit.

You're nobody.

But whatever you are –

Martin
That's what // I am.

Robert
That's what I am.

It's just that I look in the doors of these places sometimes
And wonder what the fuck's going on.
I see all those fucking queers touching each other, kissing
each other
And I think who the fuck put you lot in charge, eh?

Well you've had your fun,
And now you have to pay for it.

Because one night you think
'I can just go in
What's stopping me?'

> ROBERT opens his bag. He looks at the contents for the
> first time, emotionless.

And so that's what I did.

> ROBERT buries MARTIN.

No more.
No more feeling.
No more of them and less of us.

No mercy.
No pity.
No peace.
No love.

It's simple.
There's right and wrong.
Black and white.
Clean and dirty.

Dirty

Niggers, Pakis, Queers.

Dirty.
Men fucking men.
Women fucking women.
Black fucking white.
Brown fucking white
Until it's all, brown, brown.

And the world is just one big fucking toilet
Blocked with shit
That's gonna overflow
And drown us all.

But it's alright.
It's ok.
Because one morning, we'll wake up and we'll all be clean.
All the secret, sordid, sinful things of the night before
Will be washed away.
It just takes one man.
To set the spark.
To start the fire.
To bring the whole lot crashing down.

To MARTIN.

If nobody remembers who you are
You never existed,
Right, my friend

So how could I ever feel anything for you?

To himself.

But tonight I'll watch
The edited highlight of my life –
The cameras catching my every angle.
All these endless possibilities.
A tall man,
A short man,
A dark man,
A fair man,
And it'll seem as if this was where I was always headed,
As if I was always on this one straight path,
Like I had no choice:

Us or them
Black or white
Clean or dirty
Right or wrong.

ROBERT picks up the bag.

So this is how it happens:

A man goes into a bar.
This man.
This man goes into a bar.
To have a drink.
To have a life.
To make a little mayhem.

And as he stands in the door
He won't look left and he won't look right.
And he won't look anyone straight in the face...

He'll look like someone who knows exactly where he's going
And what he's going to do.

You'll be in there with all those bodies close to yours.
And the whole place will feel like it's dancing.
Dancing for you.

But you won't feel anything, for any of them.

Because you'll be in paradise.

In the end, it doesn't matter that it was a difficult, dangerous
thing to do.
You just have to remember that it was your destiny.
And you do it.

ROBERT puts the bag down and goes.

End.